The Invisible Disability

Gwendolyn Davis-Loyd

Editor: Sharp Editorial, LLC

Publisher: Chynna Creative Co., LLC

DEDICATION

This book is dedicated to my daughter, Jewell Loyd. This book is also lovingly dedicated to Jarryd Loyd, Calvin Loyd, Casey Loyd, Sarai Loyd, Josiah Loyd, Shirley Davis-Eves, Montie Apostolos, Gregory Thomas, Larry Davis, and Pamela Moore.

ACKNOWLEDGMENTS

Thank you, Jewell, for inspiring me to write this book. I have so much to share with parents and children of learning disabilities, and I am thankful for this chance to share in a creative capacity. I see how disabilities affect you, but I also believe a disability can serve as strength instead of a weakness. I would also like to thank my editor, Laci Swann of Sharp Editorial, for her editorial assistance.

CONTENTS

A NOTE FROM JEWEL

We are more than our diagnosis.

We are leaders, innovators, and creative minds.

We are human beings.

Embrace your differences, never be afraid to ask for help, and move toward your goals with courage and strength.

I believe in you. Now, I need you to believe in yourself.

We are difference-makers, game-changers, and the authors to our own stories.

So, ask yourself – how do you want your story to be told?

\- Jewell Loyd

Introduction

Brinkley, Illinois, is nestled in a charming area among a vibrant community in the Northshore area of Chicago, where approximately 10,000 people live. Brinkley is also within ten miles of O'Hare Airport, Downtown Chicago, and a lovely suburban school, Johnson Hall Elementary. Although Brinkley is a short distance from the hustle and bustle of Chicago, this city also has a touch of a small-town feel.

One day, Raven's mom, Linda, discovered this beautiful neighborhood while driving around and accidentally losing her way, yet this accident led Linda to immediately know that Brinkley would be her home, the place she would raise her children. Linda was eager to go home to tell her husband, Brad, about the beautiful two-bedroom Georgian home she saw on sale and call a realtor to see the house.

Brinkley was built in the early 1960s, and this town consists of grand, all-brick homes that housed upper-class families and matching incomes. Brinkley is also predominantly white with a large Asian and Jewish presence. Linda certainly did her research after seeing her dream home. She learned that the majority of the neighborhood is highly educated, white-collar workers and that real estate in this area was priced over a quarter-million dollars, but one little Georgian home stood out. Linda had discovered that an older woman happened to be moving into a nursing home and wanted to get rid of her Brinkley home. Luckily, this property was affordable for Linda and Brad. Linda, a high school teacher with a master's degree, and Brad, an executive manager with a commercial cleaning company, were hard-working, well-to-do people who had their sights set on this town.

After contacting a realtor, Linda immediately felt annoyed by his reluctance to show them the house, especially after he had met them and realized they were a black couple. As he showed them the home, the realtor continued to make comments about how he thought they would feel more comfortable in Maywood, a predominantly black suburban area on the west side of town. Brad could see the frustration on Linda's face and did everything to settle her irritation because he knew she would lose her patience with this prejudice man. Despite the realtor's comments, Linda and Brad focused on making their dream home a reality, and within a few short weeks, it was a done deal. They bought their dream home in Brinkley, Illinois, ten miles from Downtown Chicago.

Brad and Linda were elated about their first purchase together, the home where they would raise their kids and live comfortably without violence, murder, and having to bar their windows. After signing their names on the dotted line, the new homeowners decided to ride to their new house, take pictures of the rooms, and create some decorating ideas.

Around 9:00 p.m., after enjoying a celebratory dinner, they excitedly drove to their new house. As Brad and Linda walked to the front door, struggling with all the new keys given to them and trying to figure out which key would open the front door, they were blinded by flashing lights and bombarded by the sounds of several police cars.

"Sir, I need you to put your hands up," a strong voice boomed as he rushed toward the front door to apprehend Brad.

"Hands up?" Brad confusedly asked. "What are you talking about? What did we do?"

"Sir, put your hands up, both of you!" the policeman shouted again as he inched closer to the couples' faces.

Linda saw where this was going, and she feared the worst yet committed to remaining calm. "Sir, we live here!" Linda yelled.

The cop coldly walked towards them as they stood with their hands in the air. "Do you want to get the key and enter the home, Officer? It should be the key with the red ring on it," Brad instructed, visibly irritated by the situation.

"What are you people doing over here?" the cop barked without trying to mask his hatred.

"You people?" Linda angrily retorted.

The cop looked at her with a nasty glare as he tried to open the front door with the key attached to the red ring.

A few seconds later, the cop unlocked the door with ease, stepping into the foyer of the couple's new home.

"Do you have the deed to this house?" the cop then asked, demanding further proof despite opening the front door with Linda and Brad's key.

Brad looked at the cop in sheer disbelief. "I happen to have it in my hand. I wasn't expecting to have to prove my purchase, but I see it was heaven-sent that I brought it because who in the name of Jesus would walk around with their deed to prove they are the owner of their property," Brad growled, irate by the unpleasant turn of events.

The cop flippantly looked at the deed and carelessly turned the pages. He even had the nerve to ask for the couple's driver's licenses.

"This is getting really crazy!" Linda said angrily as she gathered the third piece of evidence to prove her innocence.

When the couple pulled out their licenses, the cop stepped back and disingenuously apologized.

As the officer exited the house, the lights from the cop cars continued to flash, and neighbors were nosily looking outside, trying to figure what was going on in their typically quiet neighborhood.

"Well, I guess that's our official welcome to the neighborhood," Linda said angrily, slamming the door.

Raven's First Day at Johnson Hall

Raven, a beautiful 4th grader with big brown eyes, perfectly parted pigtails, and a lean yet rather muscular frame for such a young lady, was gearing up for her first day of school at Johnson Hall Elementary. Raven was a confident and cheerful little girl, often perceived as a pretty tomboy. Linda decided to drive Raven to school for her first day at Johnson Hall Elementary School. Linda wanted Raven's transition to her new school to be seamless. As they pulled up to the front entrance of the school, there were several parents with their students, standing with them in their respective grade-level line. Linda noticed Raven appeared a bit nervous.

"Mom, are you going to get out of the car with me? Raven asked with a hint of nervousness in her voice.

As Linda watched Raven looking out the window, she noticed that her daughter was excited but hesitant.

"Of course," Linda gently responded, trying to give Raven added confidence.

Linda parked her car near a side street and walked with Raven to her respective line where the other students waited. Raven tugged her book bag strings and pulled the straps tighter to her shoulders to gain a sense of security. Parents and students stared at Raven and her mom as they walked to the 4th grade line. Linda walked very confidently with her head held high and instructed Raven to ignore the stares and walk with confidence. They could see the parents staring and whispering as they got closer to the 4th grade line. Raven then stood in line with the rest of her class when a few Asian girls, who apparently knew each other, pulled closer to one another and whispered something in each other's ears. Linda and Raven both noticed their secret whispers, and Linda immediately told Raven to ignore them. A few moments later, the teacher approached them and introduced herself to Linda. Linda extended her hand to greet the teacher.

"Hi! My name is Ms. Coby, and I'm going to be Raven's homeroom teacher," she cheerfully said.

"Nice to meet you. My name is Linda Pierce. I'm Raven's mom."

After exchanging a few pleasantries with Ms. Coby, Linda turned to Raven and said, "Okay, Raven. Mom's going to work. You're going to be alright, okay?" Linda shot her daughter a cool wink rather than sharing a hug because she didn't want Raven to feel embarrassed.

Linda had done her research about the schools in Brinkley. She knew that Johnson Hall Elementary was 391st of

2,100 Illinois elementary schools, ranking rather well. The student body was primarily Caucasian and Asian, and there were no black students, not one. Johnson Hall was comprised of 400 students, grades third through fifth, with a student-teacher ratio of 15 to one. On paper, Johnson Hall had all the pieces of a stellar elementary school, but Linda knew Raven would stand out for more reasons than her sweet disposition and outgoing personality.

Ms. Coby led her students to her classroom, and students began to hang their book bags and walk to their labeled assigned seats. Once the students sat in their assigned seats, Ms. Coby instructed each pupil to introduce themselves so everyone could begin to get to know each other. She assigned their books for the other teachers' classes and reviewed instructions, procedures, and rules. Raven was really impressed with the way things were going, especially happy about her pleasant homeroom experience, and feeling great about her new school.

"So far, so good," Raven happily whispered to herself as homeroom came to an end.

A few hours later, Raven discovered that lunchtime was structured much differently than her former school in the city. Their lunchroom was like a real restaurant!

"Wow," Raven murmured as she excitedly scanned her jazzy new lunchroom. Students were allowed a choice from the hot and cold section, fruits and vegetable section, smoothies, and treats. She was so impressed! As Raven continued to scan each section, she had reached for a tray, but one of her classmates snatched it out of Raven's hand and giggled with her friends. Taken aback by her cruel classmate, Raven gave her a nasty look, expressing her dissatisfaction with the unnecessary nastiness.

Raven sat alone during her first day, she didn't mind if

her classmates didn't want to sit with her. She knew they had their own friends, many of which grew up in the same area, as her mom made her aware of the cliques. The cheerleaders sat together, the jocks congregated at another table, and the artsy kids formed a group of their own, too.

As Raven continued to eat her lunch in peace, solo, five cheerleaders plopped themselves at her table. They were blonde-haired with pigtails and braces, very well-dressed in expensive outfits, shoes, and hairpins adorning their hair.

"Hey, my name is Alice. What's your name?" Alice flatly asked Raven, as her long pigtails draped her shoulders. Alice stared intently at Raven, looking her up and down, to see if Raven fit in according to her standards.

"My name is Raven," she responded as she continued eating, not really paying attention to them.

"I see you're wearing the latest Michael Jordan shoes.

What does your mom do?" Alice snidely asked.

Raven shot her a look as if to say, "What business is it of yours?"

"Why?" Raven finally asked, hardly masking her annoyance.

"Because you're from Chicago. How can you even afford those kinds of shoes?" Alice asked, glancing at her peers and laughing with them.

Raven, although typically quiet and even a bit shy, already had it with her awfully cruel classmates. "First of all, you're presumptuous to stereotype people from Chicago. Secondly, my parents work just like your parents work and they can afford to buy me these shoes, so get out of my face!" Raven said sternly.

Raven removed herself from the table and hurried out for recess with the rest of the 4th graders.

"Presumptuous," Alice confusedly repeated as Raven walked away, clearly clueless by Raven's choice of words.

Raven looked back and confidently said, "Yes, that's exactly what I said. Presumptuous."

Raven pulled her hair in a ponytail because she wanted to be free to play. A few guys from class were playing tag football, and Raven asked if she could play. The boys were initially reluctant but eventually agreed to let her play. That was the very moment that Raven made her name known at Johnson Hall. Raven scored five touchdowns that day and the guys on her team were jumping with joy. That was the day the "Brinkley Six" was formed.

Davis Hall – The Struggle

(6th-8th grade)

Raven settled in the district quite well. She had developed her own friendships and had become very popular on campus. She was good at every sport, winning each game she played, and she was incredibly easy to talk to and kind. Raven gained the respect of every boy on every sports team at Johnson and Davis Hall. Her teachers also liked her, and Raven began receiving national attention for her basketball skills. Every college coach heard about her and started to visit her at school to see her play. During her 6th grade year, she was so good that the coach moved her up to the 8th grade team. She was the only athlete to have played 8th grade basketball for three years. Davis Hall girls' basketball team was getting major attention from the local and national television stations. Raven had made a name for herself but not without some struggles. It wasn't until the 8th grade that her deepest insecurity set in.

Raven was struggling in her studies and didn't know why it was so difficult to master her assignments. The Brinkley Six helped Raven with her assignments; assisting her with homework, and prepping her for her tests. Raven knew something was wrong, but she didn't want to tell anyone. It took her longer to finish tests, much longer to read a simple story, and twice as long to finish a math problem. She knew the pressures were becoming more intense, and each assignment seemed to become more challenging as the year progressed. She didn't understand why everything seemed so much more difficult for her than her fellow classmates. She studied for every test and tried especially hard in math and the teachers, especially the teachers that hated athletes let you know it.

One day, Raven's teacher called on her to complete a math assignment in front of the class. Raven was struggling, yet she solved the problem her way and finally came to the correct answer. Ms. Thames walked over to Raven, squatted in front of her and yelled, "Are you stupid or something? I don't care if you answered correctly. If you didn't do it the way I said, the problem is wrong! And I don't care how good you are on that basketball court. I'm in charge of this classroom."

The other students looked astonished that Ms. Thames was saying these types of remarks. They knew Raven didn't deserve this mistreatment. All the students looked at their teacher in anger because they did not like the statements Ms. Thames was spewing. She had called Raven "stupid," and they knew that was wildly inappropriate. Worse, for Ms. Thames, Raven's classmates knew the type of family Raven came from, and the students immediately knew Ms. Thames was not going to get away with this horrible behavior.

One of Raven's friends from the Brinkley Six spoke up for her, to which Ms. Thames did not take too kindly.

"Shut your mouth, Michael! Do you want me to send you to the principal's office?" she yelled.

Michael didn't back down. "Actually, I don't care if you send me," he coolly replied. "Maybe I need to let Principal Adams know how prejudice you are, especially with my friend," Michael continued, looking at his teacher directly in the eyes.

Ms. Thames raised her arm, pointed her finger, and motioned to the door, kicking Michael out of class. As she proceeded to write him a discipline report, Raven spoke up. "You might as well write me one too because I'm calling my mom. You don't have the right to call me names," Raven firmly said.

Ms. Thames looked at Raven, revealing a bit of nervousness, now realizing she made a big mistake. It seemed as though she never expected Raven to speak up for herself. Rather than offering an apology, she handed Raven and Michael a discipline report and demanded they exit the room.

The Principal's Office

Davis Hall was the 6th through 9th grade school for the students in Brinkley, Illinois. The hallways were extremely clean and decorated with vibrant murals painted by students in years past. The restrooms looked like stalls you'd see at classy restaurants with the sink designed by an elite designer, including the motion-censors. The school also thrived with their after-school sports program. Even better, the school's curriculum was very advanced and some of their students attended a half-day at Loyola University for college credits. Brinkley took pride in their schools and the district made sure their middle school took pride in keeping it the greatest, especially without any nonsense from the teachers, staff, and students.

The incident with Raven and her teacher led to a meeting with both parties, plus the principal, the following Monday morning. Around the table was Ms. Thames, Dr. Stein, the principal, Mr. and Mrs. Pierce, and Raven.

"Good morning," Dr. Stein cheerfully said, shaking everyone's hands and asking if anyone wanted coffee or water, to which everyone declined.

Dr. Stein tried to clear the air with small talk about the weather, but Linda was not in the mood. She was there for one reason and one reason only – to speak about the awful incident that took place last week between Ms. Thames and Raven. Linda gave a dry smile but maintained her professionalism. Linda wore a sharp black business suit with high heels. Her hair was styled straight, lying on her shoulders, her nails were painted colorfully, and she wore a pair of eccentric earrings to offset her all-black outfit. The diamonds shined brightly on her ring fingers, and her aura gave off the message of refined, yet fierce. Brad, Raven's father, dressed casually yet smart, wearing his dress pants, button-down white shirt, and leather dress shoes. Brad always remained pleasant with an approachable presence.

After a bit of small talk, Dr. Stein opened the meeting. She introduced Ms. Thames and shared how long she's been a math teacher, listing her long resume of teaching experience and accolades. Dr. Stein also mentioned the importance of Ms. Thames helping to raise the math scores at this school district over the years and her history of success with students. As she spoke, Linda crossed her legs and adjusted her shoulders as if to say, "I know you're not trying to justify why Ms. Thames thinks she can get away with that type of language with my child."

Following Dr. Stein's lengthy introduction of Ms.

Thames, she then introduced Mr. and Mrs. Pierce. The fall semester had just begun. Therefore, teacher conferences had yet to take place, and parents had not met all of their child's teachers in a one-on-one setting. So, the lengthy introductions were necessary.

"Well, we will let Raven speak first and tell her side of the story," Dr. Stein said, opening the floor to Raven.

Raven smiled with a dry smile, looked at her parents, and proceeded to talk. "Well, we were in class, working on math problems, when Ms. Thames blatantly called me out of my name. She asked me to solve the problem, and when I didn't do the problem her way, even though I still got it right, she called me 'stupid,' said she didn't care that I got the problem correct and that if I didn't do it her way, the problem was still wrong. Then, she proceeded to say that she didn't care if I were a big basketball star on the court because she holds the court in her class. I don't know why she had to mention basketball because that didn't have anything to do with the issue we were addressing," Raven articulately said.

"Thank you, Raven," Dr. Stein said as she directed her attention to Raven's parents. "Would you like to respond?" she asked Linda and Brad.

"Yes, I would love to respond," Linda replied curtly.

"First, as a classroom educator, I would never call a student out of their name! That was not only unprofessional but demeaning. Think about the type of fear and embarrassment you set in a student's mind with that type of language. If I said that to one of my students in the Chicago schools, I would be fired. I would never get away with it. Not only does this behavior and language put a sour taste in a student's mouth, you are setting up a child for low self-esteem issues, especially a student who is already struggling in your class. Secondly, it was unnecessary to mention basketball to establish power in your classroom. It appears to me you have an issue with athletes, and you are making it very clear that because she is talented on the court that she is not going to get an easy pass in your class, which we certainly wouldn't expect in the first place. Your comment was unnecessary and disgusting!" Linda said angrily.

Ms. Thames appeared extremely nervous, and Linda realized tears were forming in the corner of Raven's teacher's eyes. She was turning red so the principal tried to reign in Linda's tone. She could see that Ms. Thames was about to break.

"Okay, Mrs. Pierce. If you would tone your voice a little," she said, clearing her throat. "I can understand how you might feel, Mrs. Pierce, but I've known Ms. Thames for over 25 years and she's never had one problem with any student in this school."

Raven's father, Brad, immediately spoke up, as he noticed the conversation taking a turn for the worse. "Dr.

Stein, she's never had a problem? Well, this is a problem right now. There's always a first. She's never had an African-American in her class or someone that stood toe to toe with her. She's also never had a successful athlete in her classroom. Furthermore, I don't understand her theory that if you don't do the problem her way, the problem is wrong! I don't think any educator would agree with it. As long as she can show her work, why is the problem wrong? I want to tell you something right now – don't ever call my child any inappropriate names or you will have to deal with more than me."

"I'm not going to take this abuse!" Ms. Thames said, running out of the meeting as Dr. Stein ran behind to comfort her.

Raven looked at her parents with a small grin.

"Hey, it is what it is. I'm not going to allow your teacher, or anyone for that matter, to call you names and get away with it. She can run out of the room all she wants but this is going to get settled today," Brad sternly said, rising to his feet.

A few seconds later, Dr. Stern entered the room, trying to justify why Ms. Thames rushed out of the meeting. "The tone of your voices became a little too much for her, and it upset her," Dr. Stern explained.

"Dr. Stern, and you don't think her calling my daughter 'stupid' was upsetting and demeaning, especially in front of her classmates? I want Ms. Thames to issue an apology in front of the class. If she doesn't do it today, I will have every television station at this school and have her fired!" Linda spoke with confidence, standing to join her husband.

Dr. Stein had their full attention as she wiped the sweat from her forehead. She quickly agreed to comply with the Pierce's demand for an apology. Then, Ms. Thames entered the room again and meekly apologized to Raven, to which Raven accepted.

Mr. and Mrs. Pierce walked out of the office, and the staff couldn't help but stare at them with nervous glances. Later that day, Raven received her apology from Ms. Thames, in front of her classmates. Although the meeting with Dr. Stein worked in the Pierce's favor, the word 'stupid' still rang loud and clear in Raven's young mind.

Identifying the Problem

Ms. LaRosa, a short, fair-complected woman with thin graying hair, taught 8th grade English to all 8th graders at Davis Hall. She was a beautiful teacher, inside and out, students enjoyed going to her class because she made each lesson interesting and exciting. Her classroom walls were always decorated with updated, interesting materials and a lot of encouraging quotes. Usually, middle school teachers didn't decorate their walls, but Ms. LaRosa did.

Ms. LaRosa stood at the podium at the front of the room and covered attendance. It was still the beginning of fall, so she was in the process of getting to know her students.

Students were still filing in, laughing, and gossiping with one another, some coming in late.

"Okay, everybody. You need to get to class on time before that bell rings. If you don't make it by the bell, I'm going to count it as an absence," she said. The students knew she didn't mean it but was reminding them anyway.

As class began, Ms. LaRosa passed out the Maya Angelou poem, "I Know Why the Caged Bird Sings." She asked the students to get into groups, interpret the poem and complete the worksheet.

"Whew," Raven quietly murmured, feeling a major sense of relief. "I'm glad I don't have to answer anything independently today." Thanks to the group assignment, Raven was able to escape this assignment with any embarrassment. Her studies were becoming more challenging. Raven was struggling, trying to maintain her basketball schedule and schoolwork. In fact, Raven was on the verge of a breakdown.

Linda realized she was deeply struggling with her assignments, falling behind in her studies, and failing her math class without any success in sight. In an effort to help, Linda started focusing on Raven's organizational skills, assisting her with assignments and her studying pattern. She noticed that Raven was mixing numbers, misreading letters, and developed a pattern of taking longer than her peers to do assignments. Linda conferenced with several teachers and only Ms. LaRosa agreed that Raven might have a learning disability. As an experienced educator, Linda recognized the signs and believed her daughter might be struggling with a disability.

After conferencing with Raven's teachers and principal, Dr. Stein wasn't ready to accept that someone in the district might have a disability, especially not at the prestigious Davis Hill. Instead of trying to arrange the help and assistance Raven needed, she denied her services. Through Dr. Stein's eyes, acknowledging Raven's disability meant the district would appear weak, especially if they had to provide special education services for a student with a learning disability. Worse, there was an underlying impression from Dr. Stein that Linda was merely trying to get her child an easy pass because of her rigorous basketball schedule.

Linda was livid but refused to accept Dr. Stein's "no" for an answer. Her daughter needed help, and she was committed to seeing this come to fruition. So, Mrs. Pierce went outside of the school and had Raven privately tested. After several weeks of testing, Raven was diagnosed with dyslexia.

The Diagnosis

Upon receiving the diagnosis from the testing center, Linda explained to Raven that dyslexia is a learning disability that affects someone's ability to read and that she comprehends letters and numbers differently.

"Wow, it all makes sense! Even though I understand concepts, I always had trouble when it came to organizing words and numbers on paper. This is why math isn't my friend!" Raven replied, feeling a major sense of relief, as everything started to become clear.

"I become frustrated during classroom assignments. My

friends would be done in 15 minutes, and I would still be on the first couple of problems. Teachers were calling me lazy, but I was trying my very best," Raven continued, piecing together past classroom memories in relation to her new discovery.

"Honey, you are not lazy, and you are certainly not stupid. You process information differently, and as we know, different isn't bad! Our differences make the world go 'round," Linda gently explained as she put her hand on Raven's shoulder.

After a few moments of silence, Raven looked at her mom and said, "Mom, what are my friends going to say? Is this going to change what they or my teachers think of me or how they treat me?"

Linda could see the concern on Raven's face. At Raven's age, kids are especially invested in other people's opinions. She knew Raven was thinking about the social implications of having a disorder that manifests in everyday tasks like reading and writing. She knew Raven's dyslexia would require special treatment, and although this disability isn't physically present, remaining unseen, it still feels deeply debilitating. An invisible disability, indeed.

"Honey, it doesn't mean you cannot learn or are incapable of learning. It means you learn differently. When you get the assistance you need, you will have a measure of success. Thankfully, we have the legal papers to support the services you need."

"How did this happen?" Raven quietly asked. "I enjoy learning, and I want to do well in school. Why do I have this? What does this mean for the rest of my school career and college? This feels so unfair," Raven said with tears in her eyes.

Although Linda could feel her daughter's devastation, she was determined to keep Raven feeling optimistic.

"Raven, once you get the services that you need, you

will be just fine. Trust your mom on this, okay?" Mrs. Pierce reassured. "You will receive a specialized plan that will assist you this year, in high school, and throughout college. It's actually a good thing that we know the diagnosis because now we can tackle it," Linda said, trying to comfort Raven.

Adolescence is hard enough without a learning disability. The truth is dyslexia has affected almost every aspect of Raven's life. She was ashamed, and she tried to hide it. One can only go so long before your loved ones start to suspect something, especially the Brinkley Six. They grew up together, so her friends knew something was up. Eventually, Raven told them why she was getting extra services. It took some explaining, as Raven was timid about sharing her diagnosis, but they were immediately supportive and encouraging, the way real friends react when a friend needs a hand.

With time, resources, and a positive mind frame, Raven discovered learning strategies that worked for her, and although every day at school was tough, she took out her aggression on the basketball court. She lived in the gym because that was the one place she felt most confident. Raven not only worked on her new learning strategies, she also fine-tuned her shot, ball handling, passing, and defense. She imagined game situations and hitting big shots. The basketball court was her sanctuary, and then it clicked – the work ethic she had in the gym, the emphasis of repetition and visualization, was something she could apply to her studies. Raven welcomed strategies for overcoming her disability and she worked incredibly hard to implement these into her life. Despite the name-calling, embarrassment, and confusion, Raven gained unbreakable confidence to never quit, on and off the court.

Made in the USA
Columbia, SC
29 April 2020